Date@Dal

By
Ila Singh

BLUEROSE PUBLISHERS
India | U.K.

For permissions requests or inquiries regarding this publication, please contact:

BLUEROSE PUBLISHERS
www.BlueRoseONE.com
info@bluerosepublishers.com
+91 8882 898 898
+4407342408967

ISBN: 978-93-5741-726-6

Cover design: Muskan Sachdeva
Typesetting: Rohit

First Edition: August 2023

Dedication

The author whole heartedly dedicates this journal book in gratitude with awakened sense to the awe-inspiring reflections of Dal at Srinagar; progressively guiding her overactive Mind to mind itself from the invisible entanglements so as to reach out and embrace the energy of the four fleeting seasons of life within and without.

Contents

Prologue

Dal (lake in Kashmiri language) is truly a 'Jewel in the crown of Kashmir' that graces the Indian peninsula; is the life line of Srinagar the summer capital city in Jammu & Kashmir, India. Though the physical parameters of Dal are impressive, yet they are no match to the reflections offering a breath-taking view of the mighty Himalayas silently admiring, overlooking as well as guarding Dal. My initial interaction with Dal started casually during morning walk around Dal, which gradually fascinated me for a captivating evening stroll to witness the exhausted sun signing off to submerge and merge with the generous Dal after a lengthy day.

Dal in its pristine presence and transparency guided me to explore the reason to be here away from my roots of hot humid north Indian plain during June 2020; which got me back from state of wander as to why I am here in Kashmir at this time? To be at ease while accepting this shift and wonder yes! I am here in Kashmir not as a mere coincidence of certain random facts but due to powerful alignment of various natural forces, to ensure my presence here in letter and spirit; particularly during this unique time of the year when the entire globe including the country was experiencing compulsory lockdown or curfew etc due to coronavirus pandemic declared by the WHO.

Though, the restless mind kept oscillating like a pendulum from the diverse insecure thoughts of 'what if' to be in a state of secure acceptance of 'what is'. Thus, this shift of energy from uncertainties within amalgamated with the awe-inspiring beauty of this place, which kept me engaged all day long, eagerly looking forward to getting back to my favourite spot each evening to witness a unique and special sunset with the twinkling skyline gradually merging with the mystery and stillness of a long silent night. Gradually, this as a regular habit motivated me to welcome a new day, as a 'gift', a bundle of joy for sharing new experiences that unfolded with time, consistently throughout my stay in the city of Srinagar.

Floating Garden at Dal

Dal in its own distinctive manner connected me to the fact that *'true humanness entails virtue and rejects vice'*; which is why Dal for me is a source of inspiration, joy, a born achiever; a true survivor despite witnessing all conflicting melodrama about the history of Kashmir, has till date stood as a sole witness to all the tortures inflicted by the mankind, yet imitated only the best opportunities in form of a blooming lotus garden, water lily, floating vegetable garden, fresh water fishes and so much more to the populace of Kashmir.

The presence of Chinar tree is exclusive to eastern Himalayas in Kashmir, and is also linked with the forte and perseverance of the place. A famous tourist spot known as 'Çhar Chinari' an island in the lake is marked with the presence of historically four Chinar (maple) trees from where the best view of Dal can be captured by traveling in a light, flat-bottom boat commonly called as 'shikara'.

Dal being an urban lake is an integral part of the city's prosperity, abundance and growth along with a delicate transparency and powerful reflections to convey that whatever you give to Dal will certainly be delivered back to the populace multiplied manifold. The impressive shore line of Dal has the honour to host two major practicing religions of the province; where in the wisdom of the great Hindu saint 'Shankaracharya' impeccably amalgamates with the glory of 'Hazaratbal' a respected Muslim shrine. Consequently, due to the presence of such virtuous personalities in the past have ensured that blessings keep pouring in and around Dal throughout the day even today, as echo of 'azan' from the mosques, aptly blends with the auspicious 'prayer bells' from the temple. Thus, making Srinagar truly a soulful city all day along.

The city also seizes an impressive architecture of the great Mugal rulers of India in form of Nishat and Shalimar garden built by the emperor Jehangir, Pari Mahal an observatory of Dara Shikoh, Chashme Shahi a royal spring garden built in 1632 to make the past oh so real as well as graciously alive. It's no wonder that the great Persian poet Firdausi defined the stunning beauty of the Kashmir valley as 'Jannat' in Persian language as;

"Ägar firdaus bar roo-e zameenast,
Hameenast-o hameenast-o hameenast."

This translates as 'If there is a heaven on earth, it's here, it's here...'

No wonder, the essence of the ambiance coupled with magical reflections of Dal kept me involved to share my experiences in the most simplistic, honest and humble manner as 'Date @ Dal'. As my mind learned to merge with the depths of Dal; to explore this exclusive yet enchanting opportunity provided with bounteous time and space to work on my own insecurities to eventually evolve and rise like a phoenix from the ashes of doubts and confusion. This was easy for me during the second half of 2020 as the majority of the world was still entangled in the news and views about the global pandemic issues, concerns which thankfully somehow have so far not caught my attention.

This eventually turned out to be a special phase of my life, as thoughts like clouds floated naturally across the mental horizon in alignment with Dal, providing me a robust base to be congenial with the unrestricted flow of life within and around. All this provided the desired insight to align with the natural forces; patiently waiting all around for my undivided attention; to reveal the mysteries about life in general and nature in particular. Life is good if one is not caught up in the imaginary/ unknown fear of any invisible virus, would rather be comfortable with the alms of nature to experience an extraordinary life here on mother earth.

Despite this unknown uncertain phase of life amid curfew, lockdown, social distancing, travel restrictions to my hometown, depressing news in the mass media etc; my only respite was this friendly corner on the bank of Dal wherein the soothing shades of setting sun on water, made me revisit the rabbit hole along with silent yet meaningful conversation with Dal. This provided sufficient space to quieten my over anxious mind on one hand to dive in deep with the mysteries of Dal on the other. Gradually this morning /evening routine became a regular practice guiding me as;

"The noble *minded are calm and steady; little people are forever* **fussing and fretting."**

..... Confucius

No doubt, this as an unfamiliar practice challenged my original neurological wiring of dwelling in the past to pull me out in order to be in the present. Yes, of course this was not easy in the beginning as this new habit took some time to create new neural networks as well as neural connections to reprogram the unsure mindset; to be at ease during this uncertain time. Consecutively, this as a regular practice assisted to unwind and release all consciously/unconsciously accumulated stress throughout the day gradually.

Hereafter, releasing this stress regularly created sufficient space for my intuitions to show up, reset the compass, to explore this link and its influence on different phases/ stages of human life in coherence with the four major seasons in nature. It is important to observe that each season in Nature is intricately as well as intensely intertwined to match with a particular phase of human life. Yes, these were the moments of life wherein I forgot about clock time completely, however, honouring the practice of diving in deep with Dal to understand more about the learnings from the seasons in Nature and its meaningful connection with the four major phases in the life cycle of the human being.

☆ **Paste your favourite photograph HeRE**

Describe what you like about this picture..

....

The first season in Nature is Spring which is almost identical to the cheer, joy, learning and growth as a young adult. Further, during this initial innocent phase certain basic values as a program are installed or absorbed from the external environment consisting mainly of parents, guardians, teachers etc which as a manual or as a compass exist within the individual for the entire lifetime.

A short prayer to start the journey;

" I am so delighted and grateful now that Me and _________Together in this Divine_________ Reach_________ Find__________ Count_________ here now!

Splendid Spring @ Dal

Spring young and vibrant shows up as the season of the year when the entire ambience is pink, quite similar to the initial phase of human life with the potential as well as opportunities unfolding like a humble bud gradually but consistently throughout this phase. This stage is almost identical to planting thoughts as seeds in the fertile mental soil of the child during the initial years; nurturing it carefully with complete dedication so as to reap the benefits of the harvest subsequently. Though the mind is still in its formative stage yet the primary roots of a deep seated family belief system starts germinating in the psyche of the child during this nascent phase itself without any inhibition or resistance.

Thereafter despite attaining adulthood certain belief systems, values or acquired traits of early childhood say up to the age of 7 to 9 years stay deeply embedded in the human psyche or mind-set for the lifetime. Since, the mental filters are yet to develop; hence, even minute details are absorbed and acquired from the external environment by the child as such. Therefore, this growing up phase is almost identical to a programme being installed / downloaded on a brand new mobile, laptop or computer. The child usually absorbs the attitude, behaviour and lifestyle patterns of the adults present in the extenal environment cent percent: which is likely to impact the future life of the child a 100 percent.

Children at this stage are usually given very limited options to choose from, further, the gross belief system of family including the code of conduct are not discussed with them at all. Thus, the role of mindful parenting becomes essential and pertinent at this juncture in a child's life; as this is the broad base from which life is expected to bloom in the near future. All this and much more would in turn impact the future life choices, events and circumstances etc. of the growing up child. It's therefore, no surprise that the majority of family traits including family diseases run in a family uninterruptedly as no one in the family has the time to pause and reflect on the existing invisible gaps of the family's belief system.

In and around this time in life the parents, guardians or caretakers are also introducing the child to the **'Do's and Don't'** list of the family which may be completely undetectable and totally irrelevant for the growing up personality yet meticulously seized in the young mindset without any doubt or conflict. This is also the phase where in learning, practicing, memorizing, initial interaction with the outside world starts without any alteration or deliberation as the mental framework of the child is translucent and crystal clear to acquire, absorb and adopt all that which is likely to be appreciated / praised by the grownup adults in close vicinity.

No wonder that the moments of solitude on the bank of Dal connected me to this dormant state of the acquired mind; a mind that one has regularly and warily adopted, guarded it so closely till now at every level i.e. physical, mental and emotional. At the outset certain quiescent resentments, fears and doubts start to show up all of a sudden; particularly in those delicate moments when one is a bit caught up mentally somewhere else or is occupied in some other task.

In order to correlate this, consider a situation wherein mindful parents are aware of the power of thoughts and imagination; hence, they are able to introduce this concept to the offspring easily, particularly, about the nature of the thoughts which is virtually analogous to the random floating clear white clouds of spring. Since conscious parents are able to inculcate an understanding about the presence of random thoughts in the mind-set, which on an average constitutes about 60,000 thoughts per day that are likely to visit or inhabit the mental horizon of the chirpy teenager. These thoughts are usually repetitive in nature as around 80 percent thoughts of yesterday occupy the mental space today also.

If the child, teenager or young adult is taught to pay attention to the thoughts of his / her choice, desire, wants regularly; this will enable him/her to focus on one thought at a time. This is easy to learn with undivided attention and regular deliberate practice to allow and retain the thoughts of choice; otherwise the mental horizon may remain clouded /occupied with the random, mundane repetitive and predictable old familiar thoughts. In addition, if filters are not introduced to a young adult by aware adults then the stage of 'wander' takes over the young mind-set. Therefore, it is essential that the parents, guardians, school and society are adequately equipped with desired and deliberate practices, ample patience while responding to simple issues that may appear complex for the young mind.

★ **SURPRISE YOUR 'SELF' TODAY BY UNDERTAKING ANY THREE ACTIVITIES LISTED BELOW:**

a *Take a joy ride*

b **Sign up for a new activity class for the first time**

c *Make conversation with someone 10 years older or younger to you*

d *Switch off all electronic devices to ensure no screen time for at least 8 hours.*

Therefore, it is important for the teenager to learn and think clearly so as to know the value of each thought and word that he/she speaks, as usually both the thoughts and words are downloaded and acquired only from the external environment. The parents and teachers are so much caught up in the academic performance of the teenager that usually this is neither taught by the parent, or caregivers at home nor by the school teachers / authority. Hence, this gap remains as an acquired trait amongst the majority of the youngsters during this initial growing up phase. Therefor, it is not surprising to note that the young adult during this delicate spring phase slips to the insecure wander phase easily; feels lost at times or incomplete due to comparison / disapproval from the parents and teachers while growing up in society particularly during the present lockdown phase in 2020.

Further, the children in Kashmir valley were worst effected than ever before as all the schools, playgrounds have remained closed for almost two successive years i.e. during 2019 and 2020 due to conditions beyond their control. Therefore, the children/teenagers were left with no option other than of remaining glued to the screen by either playing video game, attending to online classes or forced viewing of TV programs which are likely to impact the overall growth and development of child at this vital stage in life. In addition inviting the casual remarks of the adults all around about the youngsters of today lacking attention and focus which in turn increases the stress for the child; as no one till date has taught the child how to focus or concentrate however, everyone whether at school or at home expects the child to know how to pay attention and concentrate.

The Tulip Bloom

Consider for a moment a live case scenario wherein the child has been provided necessary opportunities to choose, to make a point, to speak and express 'Self' rather than following the instructions of adults verbatim. If a child is taught to be attentive from childhood about the value of every thought they think and every word they speak; this learning stays with them as a backend program while creating their future or painting new ideas/ views fearlessly to the world. As is known, the **'Law of Thinking'** is relevant and important for youngsters, which is identical to a computer programme, or conditioning as this is the phase to learn and practice deliberately on the law of thinking; else majority of thinking will be overtaken by the peer group, cartoon shows, movies etc. Further, the 'Law of Thinking' is a miracle to learn and work with, otherwise the fertile mental soil of the youngsters will soon be inhabited by the weeds that start germinating on its own if due attention and encouragement is not provided by the parents and teachers during this phase of life.

1. *Write down your favorite song / music, hum it, which words gel with you write here.*

2. *Play a field game of your choice preferably with your school friends*

This also appears to be the time to admire the diverse layers as well as the depth of the mighty Dal, to dive in deep with the reflections of our own eyes to genuinely connect to the inner child within. This little child has been patiently waiting for this moment, to acknowledge its presence and converse with. This is required to be practiced often to be with the inner child while admiring the depth of Dal along with the delicate scent and pink colour of the spring season here.

While, growing up during the initial spring phase the basic learning at home and school prepares the child to face the various challenges of life in future; with the desired attention and practice so as to maintain the focus on what really matters in life at any given point of time. Being able to connect to 'Self' is a germane task; which is astonishingly neither taught in school nor in college / University across the globe. Therefore, the main concern at this juncture for the parents and guardians is about accepting their own insecurities, doubts and anxiety; as

It's only when each individual takes over the task of self-ownership to be an Ubermensch (the ideal superior man of the future who could rise above conventional dogmas to create his/ her own values, originally described as Nietzsche), would mean to find the true purpose to be with the 'Self' a new start – up project now. The choice is of the individual to either be a 'Slave to your society or Slave to yourself' as if 'Self-made' or 'Herd made'.

Therefore, if the initial learning is focused on training the mind, organizing thoughts coherently then the matter has no choice but to follow the leader i.e. the Mind. The mind and matter concerns need to be discussed and taught to the teenagers regularly so that they are open to the channels of communication with the loved ones and are not caught up in the self-defeating thoughts during this initial phase of life. As a consequence, the spring of life would denote an enthusiasm to be with the 'Self' and not losing the life to the outside world, say in substance abuse, alcohol in a tavern, pub, dance club or discotheque etc.

Accordingly, this creative phase in life is all about the eagerness of exploring new avenues on one hand with desired interest and energy as a dependable and robust personality for the future or may lose interest and get entangled in the matrix of people, things and circumstances; thus wander in various prurient activities which are easily available on the internet / external world all-around. Since spring is the season of opportunities and possibilities that flow effortlessly this is the time to invest in 'Self' the greatest investment ever to guarantee the best interest in the future.

This anxious state kept me occupied on one hand while silently admiring the colourful yellow attire of Dal on the other. As this new attire is acquired by Dal due to the seasonal yellow water lily bloom, to explore about the factors or incidents that may constitute the real spring of life. Well any guesses as to what may constitute the real spring of life? Probably, the real spring grossly exhibits real freedom, as true humanness that entails virtue and rejects vice.

Yellow water lily bloom

To my understanding spring is the time in life to explore the miracles of everyday life that keep showing up / happening everywhere including the bank of Dal. Meanwhile, the day sun has left the floor and signed off, baring a small corner adjacent to the Hari parvat, refusing to sign off just like a young teenager rejecting to be with the twilight and stars amongst the silent Himalayan mountain ranges all around.

By this time the sun leaves the canvas for me and Dal to explore, as a gentle pink wave shows up and grows bigger and mightier to cover the entire surface of Dal; thereafter the pink wave flawlessly merges into the purple fringe giving an impression as if an enthusiastic under water current has shown up on the surface, like a chirpy teenager to make me explore what is in store for me here or is it the genuine simplicity of Dal to make me curious about what next; eventually as Dal transforms from a delightful pink to soulful purple all at once within a flick of second keeping my attention engrossed to this genuine genius who is here to teach me the best that life has to offer at this juncture. I am overwhelmed with such awe-inspiring beauty that presented itself for a fraction of second, to share this amazing incident here, which as a main memory is seized in the jukebox i.e. mind to be relished and revisited as and when required.

"Spring is the phase of growth the idea is to grow silently. Learn not to show off everything you have and to learn to grow in silence!

A seed grows with no sound but a tree falls with huge noise. Destruction has noise, but creation is quite.

This is the power of silence.... grow silently."

........Confucius

Alternatively, this could also be a tactic to instigate me to be here more often; so as to dive in the deep depths of my own mental illusions along with the imitation of the admiring still mountain range.

Well whatever may be the reason from Dal's point of view; however, my limited mind could link the spring phase as almost identical to the shift from the gross to the subtle; i.e. from raw base metal / an unrefined carefree teenager to transform to a more relaxed and composed adult during the summer phase of life. All this and much more depending on the type and kind of conditioning, programming an individual was exposed to or may have downloaded / acquired during the growing up phase which eventually becomes the base level backend learnings, opportunities to nurture in the future.

This is the time of the calendar year when the spring energy is all around, energy itself is such a powerful entity; can feel when it is on or when it is off, when it shifts and when it's simply not there. Therefore, like a keen learner as an honest student here on mother earth it is essential to align the energy of Body Temple with that of an enthusiastic Mind, in harmony to bloom wherever planted. In fact, this cheerful phase in life is preparing each individual to be assured and ready to experience the heat, dust and sweat of the summer phase of life more effectively.

Therefore, in sum and substance this spring phase is appropriately equipped with the choicest virtues interlinked and inter-connected with inbuilt characteristics that may be represented as learnings during the spring phase as;

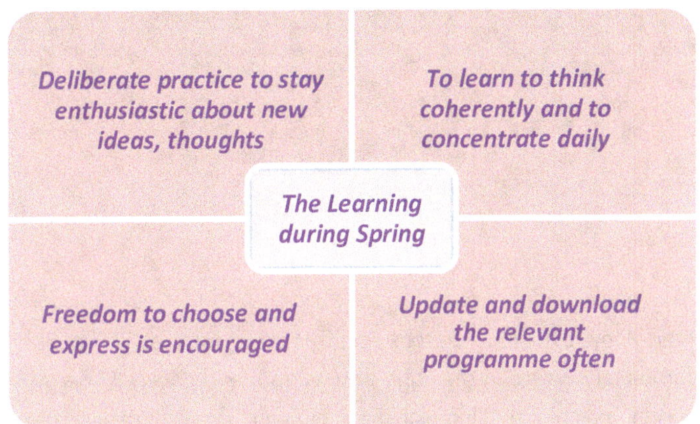

Spring is the season for deliberate practice as the core habit to capture and mingle with the joyous spring energy all around; therefore, this cheerful phase of life for an individual is a state where in the natural flow of choice overrides all limitations and doubts of the past conditioning or programming as this is the time to sing and dance in harmony with the music of fresh breeze, the chorus of spring birds melody, in tune with the school of fish in flow to achieve the perfect symphony that we are all here to experience and be with.

Gradually these fresh spring thoughts unfold and bloom in the unique scent along with freshness of life energy ready to overtake all challenges gradually yet persistently. Let the flow be in coherence with the *'Law of Learning'* with deliberate practice to focus and concentrate on one thought at a time to be with the inspiration and joy of learning as;

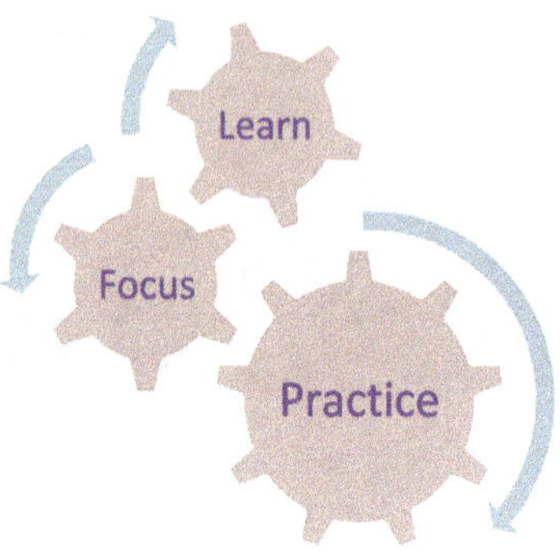

As is known, the four seasons occupy human mind as well as spirit completely where in the light, free, vibrant and cheerful energy of spring inspires the individual to be with desired patience and persistence to overtake the entanglements of the summer phase which is primarily dominated by the newly formed relationships, partnerships etc. Thus, the spring in nature at Dal connects the human psyche to the delicate phase of life to learn, practice and grow with, no matter at what phase of development the individual is at.

Appreciation certification

To whom so it may concern

This is to acknowledge, that the following qualities possessed by me……………………………… (Name)

1……………………………

2……………………………

Are here to support me and provide further guidance in accepting all the conditioning as well as the backend programming that I have received during my Spring phase.

The above mentioned qualities will guide and support me during my Summer phase and I am here to adapt to the challenges that may show up due to my backend programming.

Date :

Place :

Stupendous Summer @ Dal

As the enchanting pink spring gently transforms to vivacious green surroundings in alignment to welcome the vibrant summer season in the valley; the Dal in its glory reflects all the possible lustrous shades of green to correspond with the ambiance perfectly. This is the time of the year when the summer birds get busy exploring new relationships, preparing for the nesting phase, basically reminding the entire populace about the value of relationships in life. Therefore, being in tune with the vibration of the season which is here to unfold the trial and trump as well as the heat and dust about the newly formed partnerships/ relationships for all living beings to explore and grow with.

This sizzling summer phase is primarily about identifying, entering in, establishing, forming new partnerships aka relationships on personal as well as professional front. It is therefore important to understand that until now, the relationships are usually referred to in context with people other than the 'Self'. However, it is important to note that the basic foundation of any meaningful relationship is grossly linked to and dependent on the type of the relationship that an individual shares with themselves at any given point of time in life. This is almost identical to being open to a new song, able to dance with the diverse melodies tirelessly including the song of the bulbul (night angel) that perfectly merges with the silent mountain peaks thus creating a joyous echo across the valley. Further, the afternoon Sun in its full grandeur warms up the Dal to wake up the dormant water lilies; inviting the colorful shikara's (flat bottom boat in Kashmiri) to join in and create an almost perfect harmony to the pristine and tranquil afternoon.

Meanwhile, around this time of the year the day time gets brighter and longer, reminding about the challenges of summer time that are here to keep us engaged in flair and grace. As the afternoon sun rays diligently energize each glass blade uniformly, the Dal keeps itself completely occupied absorbing the brilliant sun rays patiently and in turn energizing its surroundings. Accordingly, the water lilies systematically unfold in coherence with the direction of the sun, greeting each sun ray to bloom; which, in turn appears as if dressing up Dal in choicest yellow, pink and violet shades. This is truly a magical moment, almost picture perfect to be captured with an overall impression as the summer phase for each individual is here to explore new opportunities, new partnership or new relationships etc. as;

A   the new relationships aka partnership are the backbone for overall growth during the summer phase of life; which gradually evolves by entering into fresh personal bonds with friends, colleagues, peer, partners, spouse, in-laws etc and much more i.e. you name it and it is there with it's distinctive responsibilities and challenges which are different yet unique from the spring phase;

B   In other words, this phase is almost identical to the caterpillar phase in the life cycle of a butterfly; wherein, each individual just like a caterpillar is focused on consumption, irrespective of the external surroundings, to discover new ways and means to consume more than what is ordinarily required i.e. munch, eat, acquire whatever is easily available say money, physical asset, property, vehicle etc from any known / unknown source.

The point to contemplate during this phase is about the invisible backend default programming, inherited or acquired from the external environment during the growing up years i.e. the spring phase of life; which are deep seated and primarily linked to the past events / circumstances. This to a large extent can be apprehended only if the concerned individual is aware and attentive of his / her own invisible back end programme aka conditioning/habit; that is, deep-seated within to show up all of a sudden from nowhere at the most crucial moments; as if some invisible buttons have been automatically pressed to switch on/off the default mode unconsciously.

✻ **Write three names that *require your attention now ;***

1).......................

2)....................

3)...................

Meanwhile, for mother nature each individual here is aptly equipped to shine bright like the summer Sun; to be a born achiever / survivor regardless of his / her visible/ invisible entanglements or challenges, that may show up now and then, which may at times adversely impact the personality of the concerned individual. Though, this in few individuals appear as a powerful and impressive character with numinous ideas and indomitable courage both at physical and virtuous level, as the core motive. However, for the majority of us here there is still a lot of scope to explore, learn, aspire and motivate each one of us in a manner so as to make our existence on 'earth school' more rewarding and exceptional.

Gift of Nature

Conversely, if adequate attention is not paid then this phase may invite an individual to adopt shortcuts in life or tempt to receive favors in order to get things done just like a caterpillar. At times, this phase may also tempt individuals to wear an invisible mask to either hide diverse insecurities or adopt an overconfident attitude under the umbrella of the EGO, which may have been acquired without the awareness of the concerned individual. Thereafter, this acquired false EGO like a shield at times may gradually drift the concerned individual from the secured 'Self' to endless complexities in life.

Hence, it is during this stressful sweat of the summer phase that our intentions like a raw core molten lava overflow effortlessly so as to somehow address the challenges of day to day life: mindfully to grow out of the caterpillar phase with an intact and humble 'Self' not only by overtaking the heat, dust and temptations linked with this phase admirably; but also to transform as an individual who is at ease with 'Self' in general and external environment in particular.

Write about three nouns in pencil that have been bothering you for some time,

a)

b)

c)

Erase the item which is not under your control, erase it completely, gently blow the residue off of the page.

Therefore, the summer phase is the time to vibrate with the frequency of acceptance of 'what is' (particularly the nouns) at that point in life rather than being anxious or stressed out about 'what if' i.e. trying to control people, things, events, circumstances etc. It is only when the intelligence of acceptance merges with the abundant poise and patience to gradually build a robust base where in the core learnings about nascent partnerships can be explored/experienced during this sizzling phase. Thereafter, such flawless alliance may manifest step by step, as a perfect professional partner / fulfilling job assignment/ a soul mate or as diverse opportunities to live the life as per the choice of the individual.

Colorful Shikara's parked at Dal

Ordinarily, we are all drawn towards individuals / professions that are at comparable vibrational level i.e. physical, mental and emotional level while entering in new relationships during the summer phase. This is like experiencing the world at almost identical level, so as to ensure free flow and perfect intermingling of thoughts, feelings and emotions; which forms the platform for the necessary growth and development of each individual. Usually, there is a common understanding for a partnership to grow and evolve in harmony and coherence due to such interactions.

The point to ponder is that we are likely to receive from the system only what we give out liberally in the form of our thoughts, feelings and actions to the system. So, our intention is the primary cause that attracts all nouns i.e. person, place, things, events etc to be in symphony with the external environment during this phase of life.

Sit down comfortably close your eyes and try to quieten the mind for at least FIVE minutes. Note down the thought troubling you during this time on a separate sheet.

Further, if the objective of an action/ doing is linked to a personal gain then certainly the matching intentions are usually flowing from the self-perceived fear within; which may in long run lead to anxieties/worry/ uncertainties etc. Therefore, the summer phase of life is here to remind us about the relationship with 'Self' first more than with anyone else in life; to be in harmony with the mind and body, rather than being with the energy draining emotions like jealousy, resentment, hatred etc at this juncture. As unless or until the 'Self' is in coherence with the energy of acceptance, in gratitude to notice the diverse possibilities; until then the real existence cannot be experienced holistically. Gradually, as we are able to unlearn more during the summer phase so as to align with the free flow of vital life energy at all levels without any physical, mental and emotional blockages inside out i.e. Wu-Wei.

Thereafter, by adopting this as a regular practice of self-observation an individual can closely notice the self-defeating thoughts that may be habitual by now. Consequently, this may gradually become the best habit to adopt so as to note regularly as to "**what is going on in the head**", observing that the individual is on track to be aware of the flow of thoughts to large extent. To understand this better let us adopt the habit of observing thoughts closely, say for 24 hours initially particularly the pattern of flow of thoughts, how intricately they are inter-linked say for example if an individual is able to hold a cheerful thought for 24 hours; then it is difficult for him/her to entertain a low vibratory thought of fear, anxiety, doubt at the same time. Similarly, if a negative thought is grossly occupying the mindset for say 24 hours then it is difficult to entertain a positive thought like enthusiasm, motivation, appreciation etc. easily. Please remember '**Thoughts are Things**'; therefore, what an individual thinks about he/ she is capable to bring about; this is a simple yet profound practice and no rocket science i.e. difficult to practice.

⚹ **Observe the patterns in the new relationship on personal as well as professional front,**

⚹ *May be you* **DRAW PEOPLE,** *get burnt out from trying too hard,*

Since, every thought and action are linked hence, they appear to operate in unison and create an equal and opposite reaction not only at physical level but also at the mental level. Further, whatever hurts other person will also invariably hurt 'Self'. Therefore, summer is the time to keep cool and meaningfully occupied by exploring new entrepreneurial skills, to guard temper, anxiety etc which may crop up just like a hail storm or tornado to finish all the efforts of past. It is only during such challenging entanglements that the mind chooses to expand its horizon, overtake its own inbuilt limitations, to be with the newly found ease, understanding and knowledge in order to overtake all the associated drama, expectations, anxiety of the external environment.

⚹ *Wander the* **GALAXY** *of thoughts and explore.*

Therefore, the summer phase is all about adjusting to a new perception, a different approach to address the emerging challenges mindfully so as to eventually evolve in a dependable, trustworthy and sustainable new relationships like marriage, partnerships etc. It is worthwhile to invest appropriately in these diverse nascent relationships as it is a blessing to have an understanding boss, a supporting peer group or an empathetic partner during this trial summer phase in life, as a precious "Gift"; else the matrix of relationships may impact an individual's physical health and optimum mental state adversely in long run.

Hence, it is necessary that during this phase while exploring relationships an individual needs to be aware and mindful about the acquired backend programming i.e. habit of the spring phase, which may require frequent updates else the operating software/conditioning may appear irrelevant and outdated to the other partner; as,

➤ Who is this changed person? Why is he or she behaving in a different and peculiar manner now?

➤ Why seek approvals for anything or everything here in my own setup/place;

➤ If the new relationships are insecure, uncertain or closed about the past issues,

➤ Trying to control or limit the growth in one form or other etc

Though the above mentioned issues may appear like an 'alien' to the partner yet they are likely to be the primary cause of indifference in long run. Unless or until such trivial issues are addressed holistically they are likely to show up initially in the physical 'Self' as stress or pain/ illness of body or mind during this phase itself. These trivial issues are small and insignificant initially, hence, are required to be resolved the moment they crop up or else they remain hidden deep within due to commitments or social pressure etc.

Otherwise, due to negligence these concerns may appear to entangle the individual almost identical to the arms of octopus around the prey, with invisible suckers sucking out the pristine life energy of the passive unconscious partner. This as an attempt teaches an individual to step out of the comfort zone else it is likely to create a lot of insecurities thus, directing the individual towards the break down point. Hence, the only way out is to resolve the issue with the new acquired deep understanding, patience, and empathy.

✳ **Write in the centre of the _circle_ the BEST _moment_ that made YOU PROUD**

✳ *Write a kind message to 'Self*

The summer in Kashmir valley also invites rain to relax, cool down and admire the magnificent feat awaiting for a spectacular display in and around Dal. Gently as the stage aka surface of Dal gets ready with Sun taking a break to let the thick, dark and loud clouds create an almost perfect ceiling of a discotheque with the natural lighting and thunder sound creating an amazing temporary dance floor on surface of Dal. Thus, making this moment awe-inspiring and numinous in countless manner where in no thing is real and permanent yet everything at this juncture is perfect, whole and complete reminding us that impermanence is the real spice of life during such magical moment.

Meanwhile, the Dal in its meditative poise gives way to the tender rain droplets to energize the entire dance floor; yellow water lilies are like floor lights adding glitter to the dance floor, in tune with the melody of the chirping birds; thus making the place alive and invigorated. Consequently, the tiny, soft water droplets take over the entire dance floor in a tap dance mode formulating new dance step lucidly to augment this mystical melody which is unfolding effortlessly, inviting all to be in tune with the dance at Dal. Temporarily, the random floating clouds pitch in to create an imaginary dome with appropriate thunder and lightning thus adding to the glory of mother nature. Subsequently, this tap dance moment is captured and seized in my main memory as a brilliant Dance @ Dal.

Completely awestruck to follow the cheerful diamond shaped rain droplets that effortlessly merge with the grace of glorious Dal, to overtake the entire dance floor. Such magical moment act as reminder .....Yes I am....!! I am here only as an observer, to connect with this amazing moment, perfectly chalked out and exhibited in its glory and grace to be in harmony with the rhythm, in symphony with the nature to absorb, attune and be with here in now.

The sole witness to this amazing moment are the silent mountain range, the swaying Chinar (Maple) trees along with few boatmen on colorful shikaras (boat) singing the divine song. All this and much more is here for me to hesitantly miss a few breath initially; to slowly submerge in the moment. This is absolutely the moment to live for, to be with, cherish and evolve with; as Dal shyly but softly whispers ... "Hey come on in; be with the dance of life, as eventually we are all only dancers here on earth school: This is the way forward to be with the joy of life, to be alive.

Meantime, the lush green Chinar (maple) tree merge with the moment and sway elegantly; with Zabarwan hill range as a silent admirer guarding Dal. Thus, adding mystery to the beauty of the place, safeguarding all the life forms whether an invisible coronavirus or the extinct mammoths: as for mother nature 'All are One'; there are no contrast no differences just harmony and bliss amongst all life forms here on planet earth along with their own unique presence and grace.

Meanwhile, thoughts as wandering clouds halt to look around the mountain top and wonder hey what is going on here? What's this preparation all about? As if almost prepared to actively participate in the divine Dal dance and merge with the fleeting nature of life in general and their presence here in particular.

Yes, this is the moment for a hesitant person like me to be an aware observer, learn to overtake all perceived and invisible limitations; that have held me for so long almost like a prisoner of thoughts with the wandering mind that now marvels to this masterpiece that is here for me to amalgamate with. To break free and be unlimited, beyond the perceived mental limitations and be in tune with the 'Date@ Dal', the vibrant vital energy of mother nature; to align with the natural forces in melody to refresh and revitalize 'Self' as if to breathe in Dal in gratitude to eventually breathe out Dal in grace: as this is the moment to live life inside out. Such moments inspire individuals to grow beyond the tailor made identity/ image of a limited physical form and reach out to explore life beyond the perceived outlook/patterns

Further, evolving with this dance of life also teaches to unlearn and celebrate life with the heat, dust and sweat of summer phase wherein the unlearning happens automatically within while interacting with the external environment. To top it all this is also the phase that exposes/ expects a bubbly adult just out of the spring phase to take up the responsibilities linked to relationships in an all-inclusive manner with desired unlearning to enjoy the abundance during the awesome autumn phase of life in future.

"The secret of change is to focus all of your energy not on *FIGHTING* the old, but on *building* the new."

..... Socrates

Therefore, this summer phase in life can at best be captured as a journey from *'wander to wonder'* as thereafter, this acquired wonder becomes the base for the autumn phase to flourish. Since this phase is exclusively about identifying, forming, building, acquiring and establishing new relationships, along with the inherent risks. Hence, it is essential that an individual is at ease with 'Self' primarily; as thereafter, all external relationships i.e. beyond 'Self' seem more meaningful and flawless. However, if we are not able to accept our own 'Self' wholeheartedly we may end up reflecting unnecessary doubts, anxiety in the external environment. As it is observed that;

> "*Not knowing where you stand in someone's life*
>
> *is an* **emotional torture.**
>
> *You don't deserve that.*
>
> *Stop settling.*"
>
> ....M. Sosa

Dal also has a small island commonly known as Char Chinari (meaning four Maple trees); however only 2.5 Chinar trees are available now to greet you as one tree has disappeared and another is still a small sapling yet to attain its summer aka adult phase as on March 2021. In addition a small habitat also exists within Dal where in the local populace maintains and cultivate seasonal vegetables in the floating garden during summer.

Char Chinari

"When you love and trust people more than they deserve, surely they will hurt you more than you deserve."

.... Paulo Coelho

Therefore, summer phase is only about unlearning the views, ideas, habits of the initial learning i.e. spring phase of life; so as to make adequate space for the relearning to take place during the autumn phase. Hence, it is appropriate to identify, acknowledge and accept this summer phase about relationships with external world not as a challenge/conflict but definitely as a new opportunity where in the adult has just about started exploring the entanglements associated with the relationships. Thus, the heat, dust and humble sweat of summer is the formative base where the lotus of awareness blooms with time not by ignoring or leaving things all together but on contrary by accepting them as such without any 'if' or 'but'.

Summer season also offers warm Sun, clear blue sky, peaceful ambience for Dal to appropriately glow with the vibrant pink lotus bloom all along overlooking all the risk and mystery of the relationships matrix *per se*.

Pink Lotus Bloom

Further, the idea of what we sow now during this summer phase would eventually be the harvest to reap during the autumn phase of life. Accordingly, it is crucial to be aware of the thoughts, words and deeds as seeds sown around this time in the mental horizon which are likely to germinate or reflect back multiplied manifold. Henceforth, any expectations from external environment for conducive growth without individual's sincere efforts are likely to act as resistance in free flow of information.

What burden / unconscious weight are you caring with you?

What can you do to leave it now.

Since, this is the time to overtake majority of the challenges carefully by selecting, deleting, ignoring, aborting the non-issues that have resided within for so long either as a conditioning or as a downloaded software programme; as now is the appropriate time to upgrade the existing version of software so as to be with the *'self+plus version'* of the relevant and desirable software. This dynamic and lively tactic will ensure that an individual lives more purposefully in the new formed matrix of relationships and selectively avoid any undesirable entanglements in the future.

Hence, to ensure this the unlearning would inter alia be like;

➢ Adaptation as the way forward,

➢ Open-ended and meaningful communication amongst partners rather than ruminating over the past / non-issues or challenges;

➢ Consider each conflict or challenge as a source of unlearning;

➢ To know when and what to hold on or to let go;

➢ Acknowledge and accept the mistake before expecting others to do so; may be due to the undesirable and invisible acquired EGO mask,

➢ Give up the habit of seeking approvals/ pleasing others at the cost of self-respect;

➢ Avoid repeating the same mistake which may have become a carried forward Habit by now;

➢ Be mindful of the company you keep during this phase; be open to change as and when required;

➢ The relationship matrix teaches volumes about life to each individual which is not taught by any counselor/ coach/ teacher/ institutions/ therapists etc.

➢ To overtake this challenging summer phase cautiously pay close attention to the surroundings as the *'Birds of similar feather flock together'* as *'Our Vibes attract our Tribe'*

Further, this summer @ Dal connects me to the *'strength of water'* wherein the power of water is absolute, to acknowledge, adapt yet flow and move on as and when required. Each challenge experienced during this phase of life is an opportunity to transform at a different level and also acquire desired strength for the future in diverse manner.

The only task on hand for an individual during this phase is being mindful, to unlearn the invisible programming carefully and completely. However, if circumstances are out of control then the task at this juncture is to withdraw 'self' completely from the situation just like a turtle in order to prevent further damage.

Therefore, this is the time *'to lie low'*, let the high tide move on, to resurface only at the appropriate time when the external circumstances are conducive. Henceforth, the wisdom of Dal conveys to understand the external circumstances by making sincere efforts to explore all the available alternatives before thinking of changing them drastically or submerging in them completely. Consequently the regular practice of patience with 'Self' can single handedly dissolve volumes of confusion from the external environment. So the lesson to be learnt during the summer phase of life is patience, more patience and more patience; eventually to be the *'Master of Patience'* as a torch bearer ready for the long run. Wear your patience like a royal robe to become invisible/ visible depending on the direction of tide.

In sum and substance summer phase is only about discovering and exploring 'true relationships' which are dependable and long lasting during this phase of sweat, heat and dust. The crux of the issue is therefore linked to the choices made while deciding on major life decisions like jobs, profession, companion etc as each one of them bring in their own limitations, challenges, entanglements and insecurities about life in general and partnership in particular. Since we know by now that life is a teacher and we are all students here on earth school to learn, unlearn, relearn with the new evolved *PPP i.e. Patience, Perception and Persistence.* Therefore, as a student it is our purpose to evolve and grow in patience, with perceptions about various trial and errors in persistence to reach the top most ladder of the relationship matrix cautiously.

Zabarwan Hill guarding Dal

This can be achieved by being mindful and open to the feelings, if any, particularly about resentment, guilt, anxiety, worry etc. so as to accept and overtake them one at a time. Thus, the lesson learnt during this phase includes being grateful for all that is, with a robust shield of forgiveness as the exclusive route to maturity now. Thereafter, this freedom of thought, feelings and expression can sail you through the most turbulent phase i.e. conflicts, trials and turmoil, with adequate space to spend some 'me' time with 'Self'.

Therefore, the motto may be like 'Yes...I am here to unlearn effortlessly, in order to create adequate space to allow new ideas to arise, and show up often. Since, 'the issues are in the tissues', hence, are required to be resolved now and not carried forward to the autumn phase. Be aware to not repeat the same mistake over and over again; to evolve, unlearn and grow out of the matrix of relationships just like the summer Sun beyond the entangled clouds. Gradually, this PPP with adequate practice becomes a shield aka strength towards 'Self-empowerment'.

As life gives each one of us abundant chances to connect and discover our own presence here, where in family members, colleagues, friends etc pitch in as teachers at the appropriate time, may be only for a short duration to either learn from then or unlearn and let them go. Since the summer Sun is now shining brighter than usual, is here to teach us to shine brighter than ever before both in letter and spirit.

As such this is the time to hold the fear aka bull by the horn so as to identify, know and address all the inherited or acquired fears holistically. This is an invisible debt of the family that each individual carries unknowingly to either get sucked in or to consciously choose and dissolve the clouds of doubt and confusion. The choice is to either remain fearful and wander or be mindful to overtake and wonder. Since fear may initially appears as a block or burden; however, with regular mindful practice one can consciously choose to handle one fear at a time to be out of the nexus / web for once and for all. Consequently, individual may note that overtaking fear one at a time strengthens the mind, balances the persona as;

"That which does **not kill me** makes me STRONGER."

Friedrich Nietzsche

In addition, the external environment is the perfect teacher to stay connected to the thoughts, be present and aware of the life forces around. Therefore, the time has arrived to pay undivided attention and honor **"Self-worth"** to focus all the available energy on creating a better version of 'Self' rather than staying stuck, helpless and blaming it all on external factors or conditions.

As by now it is known that the spoken words are powerful, they stay in the Universe to come back at the precise perfect moment to create a unique world here; hence, aspire to;

Be in the **moment**

Be the *moment*

Be moment

Be

Be *light*

Be **the** **light**

Be with the light!!!

Learn to be more flexible during this phase as physical flexibility is fitness, mental flexibility is common sense and emotional flexibility is healing. The journey of healing starts during this phase itself, though in the reverse order i.e. starting from invisible emotional healing by focusing and practicing to be non-judgmental, to be with mental healing by practicing patience with Self and others so as to attain visible physical healing which sets in as the uniform *'Wellness Mission'* thereafter.

Sizzling summer phase also exposes an individual to say a polite yet firm NO when required or else the caterpillar will not know how and when to stop consuming more than what it's carrying capacity is. Therefore, the summer phase is the perfect time to identify and release all the baggage that the 'Self' has unconsciously accumulated all along, by putting aside 'Self' at the most crucial and demanding juncture with a thought;

"Thy will be done *that is* BEST for me"

Thus, the insecurities and challenges of this summer phase teach each individual patience, perseverance and persistence to overtake the ruminating thoughts of past conflicts and doubt beyond the consumption pattern of a caterpillar and be at ease with the insight and introspection process during the future, exploring the self comfortably in the cocoon to untangle the issues, unlearn from the mistakes of summer to relearn and glow during the awesome autumn phase.

Awesome Autumn @ Dal

This awesome phase in life shows up instantaneously after the heat, sweat and dust of summer phase has more or less settled; providing sufficient space for the fascinating rust color of mother nature to seamlessly merge with the profound gravity of an open, expanded and balanced mind set. As around this phase of life an individual may be still reflecting the ideas / views of past learning or unlearning, absorbed and acquired during the spring as well as the summer phase. However, a generous topping of individual's own perception about the *3C's of life i.e.* **make a choice**, *take a chance to be the* **change**, with adequate adaptation according to the Darwin's Theory of evolution i.e. *'Survival of the fittest'*. This appears to be in flow with gradual transmutation, inevitable alterations that provide an individual a dependable platform for necessary support and guidance for the vital evolutionary forces to overtake the psyche during this awesome phase.

Autumn is a second spring when every leaf is a flower

Albert Camus

Meanwhile, around this time of the year the atmosphere here has undergone a significant change with decreasing duration and intensity of the Sun during the day time, thus, progressively providing more space for the colorful evening to set in a bit early. Thus, giving an impression as if the vibrant orange yellow ball i.e. the evening Sun is tired, hence, is sluggishly taking off the boots to chill and hang out more on the other side of equator now on; thus providing abundant space for a relaxed yet stimulating twilight to set in a bit early. It is imperative to notice the vibrant colors of the setting Sun offering an entirely novel, lively but distinctive attire to the Dal every evening.

In the Indian tradition the evening time is considered sacred, hence, set aside for the prayers and hymns for all whom we owe our gratification of the day to, which inter alia includes mother nature, the deity, the loved ones etc uniformly. Personally for me this happens to be the most enchanting time of the day, as around this time the glory of the Dal transforms altogether to yet another exclusive level for any spectator to get enthusiastic about, as;

"When we reflect on the past, we recognize the struggles we never thought we would ever get through. The accomplishments we didn't know we could achieve; the breakthrough that came from some of our hardest moments, when we reflect on past and where it has brought us; we can allow it to bring in some peace to our current struggle. To remind us of our own strength, our own resilience, our own determination. To remember that the times when we are in the midst of struggle are followed by the times where we blossom once again."

.... *Tory Eletto*

Successively, the evening steadily metamorphoses with the pious echo of azan pouring in from the mighty Hazratbal Mosque on the bank of Dal to impeccably mingle with the hypnotic evening arati i.e. prayer bells from holy Shankaracharya Temple; thus, providing a 'soulful' ambiance to this place. Subsequently, this awe-inspiring sound mix takes over the entire atmosphere in its marvelous grip wherein each and every moment becomes alive and sacred in coherence with the surroundings.

Hazratbal Mosque

This impeccable evening occurrence has an empowering as well as overwhelming experience to be with, feel it; yet, not easy for me to capture this magical moment in absolute words as such, on the contrary it is easy to be in harmony with the environment completely; to grow with it a bit more each day so as to be in sync with the splendid beauty and seize this moment in the main memory forever.

Simultaneously, mother nature in its unfolded mystery and bounty is totally occupied in preparing the ambience for the fall season; which in turn teaches us the intense lesson of the season to 'Let Go' unconditionally of all anxiety, doubts, fear of past etc.

⭐ *Write down* the three **fears that** hold you back ;

a)...

b)...

c)...

As the warmth of the day signs off a bit early, thus inviting individuals to hang out and be with the fresh and crisp evening chill. Further, few new visitors are here i.e. the 'Fulica Eurasian Coots' also known as Common Coots (Kolar in Kashmiri); the migratory birds to join in and exclusively enjoy the ice cold water along with the mystery of night without any human intervention at Dal.

Playful Common Coots at Dal

Thus, this autumn phase in life is like a 'U turn' from any/every situation wherein an individual is required to be independent of all entanglements, if need be, take a selfie, as a proof to revisit and comprehend the past challenges with the new acquired outlook. This is almost identical to picking up all the broken pieces of old 'Self' with a new awesome balance to reassemble the 'Self' afresh. To relearn and know for sure **'what to assent and what to let go' as;**

"Autumn teaches us how **beautiful it is to let things Be as they are or** *Let them Go for once and for all!!!*

As such, autumn is also a rap up phase of life wherein each individual may opt to introspect; so as to eagerly bid goodbye to the caterpillar phase of life, which has all along kept the individual entangled in the matrix of wants, desires, cravings etc including all available random consumption patterns. Nevertheless, this is also the time to have a second look at the learning patterns of the spring phase coupled with the unlearning concerns during the summer phase. Therefore, as the process of introspection steadily starts around autumn phase, the 'pupa stage' sets in, wherein the desire to consume like a caterpillar has automatically disappeared, thereafter, the entanglements of external environment also lose control, as nothing really provokes or generates anxiety. Therefore, in sum and substance during this awesome autumn phase, for the first time amongst majority of human beings peace peeps in to remind that **'Peace within guarantees Peace without'.**

As a consequence, an individual learns to be at ease with 'self' despite being surrounded by external chaos; yet, feels more secure and sure; which may thereafter grow as well as glow as a genuine 'Self' confidence.

☆ Identity the activities that help in improving your Mood;

a)

b)

c)

☆ Who has the power to dampen your Mood

a)

b)

c)

☆ Try to minimize it's influence now on.

Henceforth, this is the phase to gather 'Self' carefully; which in turn provides adequate space and energy to effectively deal with the new challenges coupled with desired awareness to know what is going on upstairs i.e. in the Head, to be able to withdraw and divert 'Self' to contentment rather than staying entrapped in the **"Do's or Don't"** rule book. Thus, the singular requirement of this autumn phase is to be comfortable with 'Self' just as it is, no 'if's' no 'but's', just the "suchness" of self-acceptance, self-discipline; self-actualization which now starts to unfold slowly. This is certainly one of the most relevant and comforting phase of life as it is all about strengthening the 'Self', celebrating the uniqueness of 'Self' so that the chill / cold / freezing winter phase of life is comforting and satisfying.

Autumn and Spring seasons are quite similar yet distinct, as during the autumn phase a lot of heat and dust has settled and the clarity of presence has sharpened: to be with the reverse trajectory movement aka the reverse movement of planet earth; which is quite similar to the reverse of spring phase for the human being. Autumn phase also guides us to be humble to know from where we started i.e. to share and give back to the society from where we have acquired and accumulated possessions during the summer phase for material comfort. Thus, this autumn phase of life in which I am guides me regularly towards simplicity, desired dedication and devotion to be with the source, the life energy within; accompanied by self-knowledge, followed by self-realization to eventually glide towards *'Self-Mastery'* during the still winter phase.

The idea here is to mingle and flow with Nature, be in nature more, to be with nature; be as natural as possible, just like mother nature who does not require any makeup to cover the flaws; where the scars of life are confidently displayed or worn on sleeve to be uniformly displayed for all. Therefore, with this regular and deliberate practice to connect with mother nature at all levels with an open mind for abundant support and guidance to heal unconditionally at all levels effortlessly during this phase.

Subsequently, this is automatically taken over by the in-built intuitions; the intrinsic compass aka a trusted friend within; to be with the Miracles of life here. Once this clear connection is established, which thereafter grows as a habit, as if logging on to this intense and reliable network at any given time from anywhere for holistic healing of 'Self'. Thus, the essence of relearning defines the autumn phase completely, just like Dal in its flawless tranquil 'Self' connects as well as reflects the depths; as

"Every thought that shows up, to the feeling it creates,

Guiding to the words that show up to go along with accompanied action,

yes….

All of the above in one form or other bears your signature,

To echo the brand, that you are;

Be diligent!

Your brand is your choice, learn to choose well; as during this phase of life; every thing here is actually nothing i.e. 'O' without a twist '8' i.e. infinite as,

Around this time a friendly eagle couple has opted to undergo the pupa phase, a major change in the life cycle of an eagle, involving an intense process lasting for about 5 months say around 150 days. This process is sublime as well a fascinating, as it sets in when the eagle is about 40 years old and the eagle's long and flexible talons can no longer grab a prey essential for the bird to survive. In order to be back to normal flight routine the eagle has to adopt 3 C's of life i.e. to make a CHOICE, take a CHANCE to either go through a painful process of CHANGE, or to starve and eventually die.

Yes, this couple is quite clear in it's choice and has opted to live a life of average local birds, to be grounded and eat whatever is available in order to undergo through the painful process of initially breaking off its beak; thereafter, wait patiently, till the new beak grows back. It is only after this is completed that the second painful process will start wherein the eagle is required to pluck out it's own talons one at a time; wait for talons to grow back: thereafter, the eagle is further required to pluck off its old-aged feathers so as to make the extraordinary famous flight of rebirth, to return back to life to live for another 40 years thereafter. Thus, the animal and the plant kingdom is the real inspiring force to accept, honor and undertake the 3C's willingly so as to survive and live life like never before.

A) WRITE DOWN ONE BIG MISTAKE YOU MADE OFF LATE SAY THREE *months back*

B) Why is it not such a Big deal today

The point to ponder is that if an eagle can willfully undertake a life saving as well as life changing decision at the age of 40, then what prevents a human being to be more open to accept major demanding changes in life. Subsequently, willing to introspect, embrace and adopt the life changing cocoon phase during the autumn phase so as to eventually emerge out of the chrysalis phase like a colorful butterfly or to soar like an eagle higher than ever before.

Thus, this vivacious autumn phase teaches us to relearn, identify, acknowledge and accept change whole heartedly in order to go forth with all the enthusiasm, to let go of all limiting beliefs, open up and expand the mental horizon just like a parachute in wonder rather than wasting time to wander; to soar higher than the eagle and be more cheerful than the butterfly. As such all individuals have an important challenge, concern or issues to address and overtaken systematically which thereafter becomes the unique and desired identity during this phase. The lesson to be learnt during autumn is about the 'Change', as there is no need to be afraid of change rather acceptance of change is tangible intelligence.

Consecutively, the friendly eagle couple flies over to the nest on the tallest Chinar tree top, to break free from the mid-life blues; as the power of rejuvenated wing is with them now and they have willingly surpassed the challenges gradually; to once again overtake the small talk that small birds are entangled in and be with their choice i.e. the chance to fly over and above the cloudy sky to the new horizon where the Sun never sets; this is the spirit to be with which would in turn be referred as to fall a number of times yet be assured of 'Self' to rise and shine like never before after each and every fall. This in authenticity is the brain power aka mental power which by regular practice is now build up almost like a muscle to display it's strength in gratitude and humility. As the strength in the wings, talons, and beak is sufficient the friendly couple flies up, around and above the mighty Dal to catch a fresh carp once again bon appetit.

Since one has been observing this eagle couple for some time now; this change is an output of deliberate practice and patience all along which they proudly display now as the mighty wings are once again energized to gracefully soar, over the entire length and breadth of the mighty Dal in one stroke easily. Therefore, with the newly acquired feathers, stronger talons, a brand new robust beak, the poise and pleasure of being in the sky ceaselessly, to descend only when the perfect prey of their choice shows up.

Thus, reminding that when the desired strength of mind has been achieved despite the daily challenges for survival, only then can the power of the mental wings overtake effortlessly, soaring higher than ever before in the meditative state. Therefore, this friendly eagle couple taught me the art of being present, observant and aware to spontaneously shift the attention as and when required, being open to the core fact and the essence of life in general coupled with relearning during the autumn phase in particular.

Subsequently, this becomes a point of convergence between the autumn phase and the spring phase, as the relearning does not happen in isolation but with reasonable unlearning experience. This is the charm of the autumn phase where in the old skills are transmuted only after giving due diligence and attention to the heat, dust and unlearning of the summer phase. In the meantime, the newly acquired vision is sharp and crystal clear without any illusion or confusion.

Thus, the matrix of relationships throws open new understanding, the clarity of inbuilt intelligence, wisdom of the presence as the core innate strength of unconditional acceptance; in flow with the relearning phase, which is insightful by now.

★ ***Recall*** *all people who are with you* *no matter how many* MISTAKES *you made. Write their* **names** *here;*

a)   b)

c)   d)

In sum and substance the four major and diverse seasons in the Nature provides an impression of a 'cascading effect' or 'Waterfall effect' to connect with the energy of joy and enthusiasm once again. Thus, reminding that whatever happens is not in isolation but is interlinked like the flow, as nothing happens in isolation or as a mere coincidence. Hence, the autumn phase is for introspection to;

- Identify reasons that may have led to challenges or sufferings,

- Know what to choose i.e. to suffer or to relearn and to 'let go' of all trivial issues unconditionally,

- Inculcate the habit to talk to 'Self' often, particularly during the waking up time to seamlessly connect to the inner radar i.e. intuitions;

- Learn to quieten the mind regularly to establish an inner coherence, an emotional balance which is the new acquired strength now;

- Be aware of the chosen path, to be able to move on as per the choice that has brought 'Self' to this relearning phase during autumn

- Be open to identify, accept or let go of all what did not work

- To know if the original umbrella of trust, faith and attentiveness is on or off

- What is that an individual knows for sure

This autumn phase also teaches to acknowledge all the wonderful companions, partners, family members and friends who have stood by till date as a dependable support all along. Therefore, the relearning during this phase is primarily dependent on all unique and special persons or individuals as teachers who crossed our path and the significant role they may have played in bringing out all that was dormant within. As what we see in others exist within: hence, it is our choice to look for the best in others in order to connect to the best within. Therefore, this autumn phase teaches to recognize that *'what you sown today is what you shall reap in future!'*

☆ **LOOK FOR** something *awe-inspiring* that *you might have been* **ignoring** up until this moment. Write it down on a separate **note sheet**

Thus, autumn phase is all about sharing and caring as by now all the Chinar (Maple) trees have changed their outfit from lush green to golden yellow / shades of rust; all of them are decked up stylishly along the bank of Dal to reflect and merge with the seasons call to welcome 'the fall' season. The mighty Chinar has no desire to be in any other altered shade now; as they are in complete coherence with the deep red / rust color with broad dried leaves, in tune to celebrate the fall i.e. to let go of all that is no longer required during the winter phase of life, probably this is the reason for the fall season to be so spellbinding and captivating. The Chinar tree does not recall the summer days that kept them occupied all day long just like a caterpillar consuming, and growing, instead they are still and grateful for the newly acquired seasonal attire.

As can be observed the mother nature is unvaryingly with the congruence of the season wherein there are no comparisons of any kind either at physical, mental or emotional attribute. Nature is present and alive to accept unconditionally all that was, is and will be; without any resentment, comparison, criticism of any kind. It is indeed a blessing for me to willingly participate with the spectacle of the season, as a sole witness. admiring this enchanting rusty get up at Dal astonishingly. Thus, this acceptance of all that was in the past in general and 'Self' in particular makes this fall season so enthralling and breathtaking. Thereafter, the way forward is to pay close attention to all that is, no looking back, to be present and aware to smile at all the past challenges.

☆ In which Role Do You Shine Brightest?

☆ In which **ROLE** Do you **STRUGGLE** Most and WHY?

☆ ARE you being Too Hard on yourself? Explain.

In any set up whether at home, workplace or society there is usually an invisible yet clear power lobby under operation which is subtly guiding the majority of the individuals to 'Do' or 'Be' an active participant of what the group is promoting. This practice existed in the human society historically; usually expressing itself as EGO, had overtaken the psyche of certain rulers like Stalin, Hitler etc in the past and also being practiced by certain individuals till date.

Therefore, during this pupa phase the invisible cocoon teaches to relearn, rewind, reprogramme and update the existing software/conditioning; which only few courageous individuals are able to adopt and accept holistically. As a result, this is the time to exclusively converse with 'Self' to detach 'Self' from the unnecessary conflicts, anxiety, stress, confusion etc; to prepare 'Self' to override all unwanted insecurities.

Thereafter, trusting 'Self' is the dependable link to connect to the inner compass which is in fact the gateway towards true liberation/ freedom from insecure thoughts, feelings and emotions forever. This is the sole force to guide an individual during the still winter phase towards **"empowerment and enlightenment of Self in general and humanity in particular."** Hence, it is only when an individual is open to relearn, identify and notice the insecurities which may have existed within all along, to plug the loose ends; so as to accept them, to eventually overtake them one at a time to Let them GO. permanently Yeah!!! reminding to **RISE LIKE A DRAGON**.

Therefore, in sum and substance the relearning from Dal during autumn phase is all about self-realization and self-discovery; to connect to the intuition, the only compass to guide us through the rough weather during winter phase of life.

The idea is to cherish and celebrate life not only during certain special occasions like festival time etc. but every day and every moment to be alive and explore the new oppurtunities available to resolve the external issues. Be open to know the fact that yesterday's hard work is today's celebration. Since it is known by now that, 'what goes around in the universe; comes back multiplied many fold' as an experience during this life itself, as there are no coincidences or debt, as per the Universal law under operation.

✴ Describe what is happening with in you and around you

Gradually as the process of self-exploration sets in to understand that each one of us have a distinct yet different role to play here; wherein, whatever is good for individual 'X' may not necessarily be same for the individual 'Y'. Therefore, the entire focus during life is about learning, unlearning and relearning at our own unique pace without expecting anything in return; however, appreciating all that crosses our attention. It's only after this churning that an individual can grow out of the chakravyuh or the spider's web or the mayajal i.e. the cocoon during this lifetime itself to eventually heal 'Self' inside out.

Usually, the autumn phase relearning is broadly under following parameters;

➢ To look beyond the physical, mental and emotional challenges of today and be with the thoughts as seeds alive and germinating in the nutritious and nurturing mental soil;

➢ To make mistakes, however, avoid repeating the same mistake which is possible only if individual is open to learn from the mistakes of past; else it is likely to become a habit if the same mistake is repeated over and over again;

➢ Learn to identify, mitigate, address risk to relearn and grow;

➢ Let Go more each, day to make space for new ideas or learning to showup

➢ Connect to the enriching thoughts of today that are likely to create a valuable 'Human race' for future;

➢ The self-discipline practice of today is likely to bloom to make the winter phase more contended and satisfying.

As one adapts to be in tune with this autumn phase of life so as to learn to ignore, forgive, forget and Let Go of all that is not relevent today with a sole purpose to set aside the unconscious baggage of yesterday that one has been carrying unconsciously all along. To congregate the light within that is present in all of us to show the way forward to welcome the simple, pure, humble and wonderful winter phase in life, where the physical and mental activities are in complete coherence to shine out louder and brighter because of the light within. Thereafter, this light within sparkles to energize the 'Self' completely despite the impermanent reasons and seasons here on planet earth.

A) THE LAST DREAM YOU REMEMBER, WHAT WAS IT ABOUT ?

B) WHAT EMOTIONS DO YOU ASSOCIATE WITH THAT DREAM?

C) WHAT WOULD YOU WISH TO DREAM TONIGHT?

Wonderful Winter @ Dal

Winter with it's inbuilt quietness is also associated with the infinite source of insight and introspection; the desired direction to be with during this elixir phase of life; the elixir of immortality; also referred as **"The Rosarium Philosophor"** i.e. the philosophers rose garden commonly called as the philosopher's stone. Fortunately, philosophy is not some idle pursuit restricted for only few, rather it is the robust base, identical to a dependable spinal cord of a human being; to engage in often particularly during this wonderful yet silent phase of life. Since, philosophy assists in sharpening the outlook of an individual as well as working on with various available alternative practices for improving the life skills: which may eventually guide an individual to be in sync with all as ONE life form here on planet earth with appropriate synergy of sharing and caring.

Consequently, this mindful presence is equivalent to the chisels; wherein an individual with the desired focus and undivided attention

sharpens the mindset as if *'We set free the angel in the Marble'*

as per Michelangelo's paraphrase. Since life is a journey from the time of birth to death; so whatever happens in-between is only a treasure of rich experiences, long lasting memories, leisure pursuits which under common parlance reflects as a unique and special life for each living being here. Therefore, with this as the core backend theme it is essential to reflect all acquired learning, unlearning and relearning essentially as;

During ancient times some popular ingredients like mercury, sulphur, iron, copper and honey were used by alchemist as a recipe to create the tonic for life commonly referred to as the 'elixir of life'. Therefore, the vital role for an alchemist during ancient time was linked to transmute the basic raw material like iron with appropriate exposure to high heat and pressure, which would gradually transform the raw gross metal i.e. matter to a precious and exclusive pure 24 carat gold metal.

Similarly, the human transmutation process has also been observed due to the shift in individual's awareness to a more refined and fine-tuned presence. This, thereafter can be compaired to as 'elixir'; a well identified process where in the gross raw persona; similar to any base metal like iron along with certain specific identified art of living practices like meditation, mindfulness etc identical to glossy fluid metal for example mercury may eventually transform the raw persona of an individual to a sparkling shinny glossy gold. Thus, creating a transmuted personality to guide an individual towards alchemy i.e. modern chemistry with psychology to create the elixir of life, which in it's core state is only about the creative infinite presence i.e. awareness.

☆ List 3 ways *that you have grown as a* **PERSON**

a)...

b)...

c)...

As a consequence, on entering the winter phase of life, the raw persona of an individual has undergone a steady yet significant transformation, which thereafter, reflects as a clear shift from the raw base mental state during the spring phase, with adequate exposure to high heat, sweat and stress of summer phase. All this and much more is observed with mindful practice of introspection during the autumn phase so as to reach a state where in the presence of an individual is comparable to an illumined 'Self' i.e. pure 24 carat gold; wherein the reactivity with the external environment is visibly altered to a non-reactive or a least reactive state during this winter phase. Further, the echo of this transmuted individual is equivalent to the elegance, sparkle and brilliance of a solitaire embossed in gold forever.

The catch here is to still continue diving in deep within to effortlessly resolve all confusion, worry and chaos of external environment systematically one at a time, for if this is left unaddressed, it is likely to create certain neuro-chemical turmoil within the Brain i.e. the biggest pharmacy in the world.

Conversely, in the present day circumstances with social media and internet creating a collective hype, the aforesaid mental state could also be linked to the state of mind that has by now reached more or less a tranquil state just like the serene Dal so as to be at ease with 'Self'; to endow the seeker to quench the thirst of eternal life or be the source for eternal youth aka elixir identified to cure all diseases. Thus, during the present circumstances this desirable tranquil, calm, composed and stillness of a balanced mind is identical to the true and trusted elixir of life. This mental state can be attained easily by adopting regular meditation or other alternative art of living practices.

Further, around this phase if any individual by default has consciously not yet adopted the practice to manage the Mind effectively i.e. beyond it's perceived dramas, anxiety, fear etc; is likely to be exposed to certain challenging issues both at the physical as well as at mental level as a symptom of a physical or mental disease as the *Issues are Invariably in the tissues*. This is the real live wire life experience, teaching us to relearn and also adopt the practice to trust the process along with time 'as such'. Moreover, a closer look at the word 'disease' when broken to two words would be as 'dis' + 'ease' which would mean that the Body Temple is not at ease, hence, the visible or invisible symptoms may as a disease of Body Temple or Brain or both may appear or show up in long run.

It is also possible that these words may not make any sense to you at this juncture while you are reading the text; relax and be sure that the timing of the various events related to people and circumstances are unique and special for each individual here to learn, explore and grow with. Since, this phase is only about achieving a coherent inner state for any individual wherein the inner state or the Individual's mindset is unique and has no relation with anything or anyone outside in the external environment. Henceforth, whatever is unfolding at this juncture is a new lesson aka learning, giving an impression as if up till now the individual was being prepared for this interesting and exciting interphase: wherein each moment is meaningful as it is adding to the process of 'Self' growth and actualization.

As is crystal clear by now that we all are only *work in progress* 'to say the least or merely **'unfinished products'** till the end, and the sooner this realization about the transient state trickles down to the awareness level, a coherent and holistic state of existence is difficult to perceive and achieve.

☆ ***Imagine looking back at your life from a ripe old age, or looking down at your life from a million miles away in space***

1) **What would matter most ?**

2) *What appears* SMALL AND INSIGNIFICANT **from here?**

Another issue to be conscious of during this wise winter phase of life is the hidden cost of the acquired accumulations; which would include all physical possessions, assets etc along with the invisible carried forward thoughts which occupy a significant space and place in the psyche of an individual. Please remember whatever is free to a common persona usually has an invisible and inbuilt carry forward cost which may include the social media, internet etc. thus reminding;

"Man know Thyself." ....Socrates.

Accordingly, this winter phase is all about self-awareness with seamless intuitive guidance to be with the unique and pure source i.e.

breath. Thus, permitting the light spirited and light hearted individual to look beyond the relearning experiences of autumn phase; being comfortable in not knowing 'what next'; rather being at ease with the newly acquired self-awareness completely. This, would in turn eventually guide the sail of the ship i.e. the individual to the desired direction, assuring persistently to give up all the wanders of the past and be with the wonderful winter now. Progressively, this stage of self-awareness, as an astuteness nurtures and glows in the persona of an individual who has all along till date waited to experience life full circle. Therefore, the sole purpose of this chilly, still phase is to slow down and be with the external environment: just like Dal to freeze with the moment and acquire a new outlook as the frozen Dal.

Frozen Dal

Though the core objective / purpose for an aware and conscious human being since time immemorial is to master the 'Self' particularly in case of those who long to feel and live with the divinity. Such individuals need to be cautious and clear about how much or how little to mingle or to retract from the vanities of life in general and the external environment in particular. As any hostile, insecure, unpleasant thought is required to be processed effectively and overtaken with a regular practice of gratitude and forgiveness.

Therefore, the prospect of being in harmony with the 'oneness' of all that is in abundance here would basically mean being 'one' with mother nature which is aptly captured by the omnipotent reflections of Dal expressed in the simplest yet effective manner. Since, this is in alignment with all living beings including human beings to adopt a regular practice to explore and merge in the secure lap of raw and unaltered Nature of which Dal is also an integral part.

✮ Explore the ways in *which you can make other* people's life easier or better

Otherwise, there is no way out for human race or an individual who is caught up, rather unknowingly entangled in the diverse illusions aka maze of life; which in India is commonly referred to as mayajal / chakravyuh or the spider's web; whatever name is assigned to such entanglements; eventually it is only a matrix of person, place, things or events, collectively referred to as 'noun' in English language. Henceforth, with the awareness of 'All is One' as 'One is All' being uniformly applicable as a simple yet profound Universal Law exhibited gracefully in the external environment including Dal.

Further, it will be crazy enough to want to face difficulty in life voluntarily; however, it is equally crazy to pretend that worst is not going to happen. Let us be prepared with the appropriate mental framework and ready to submerge and reemerge as and when required. Meanwhile, this wishful winter phase is all about freedom and uniformity; as the pupa emerges out of the chrysalis stage of butterfly, this is identical to the freedom from the cocoon of old habits, patterns and behavior; to eventually emerge as a light, vibrant and free individual capable of spreading cheer and joy all around in it's raw, nascent state and not specifically made up to suite any particular occasion/ event.

Therefore, winter with its persistent stillness of mind connects an individual to an important Universal Law which also happens to be the first Hermetic Principle i.e. *Universe is Mental.* Mind is an invisible yet unique asset to assist each individual; with it's inherent yet exquisite power; all set to bloom wherever planted expressing itself, almost similar to the flowering of human awareness.

Consequently, around this challenging phase Dal has taken a call to absorb chill inside out, be with it and freeze along with the external environment so as to be in sync with the surrounding; wherein all are uniformly decked up in delicate, soft white color attire. This syncronicity adds up to the story of the *Frozen Dal* ; this rare sight is vissible now only after a long gap of almost two decades, thus taking over the headlines in print as well as visual media during the 'chillai kalan' duration in January 2021.

Man standing on Dal

This for me is a major lesson from the Mother Nature to be in flow, in sync with the call of nature neither resisting nor fighting but being with the synergy and in the moment to freeze, in turn acquiring a completely new outlook as if a new Avatar is exhibited for the populace of Kashmir by Dal now. Thereafter, keeping pace with this new avatar of Dal a modified pattern emerges wherein people are walking on the surface of mighty Dal, tourists are occupied taking pictures of this rare sight, children opting to play hide and seek, run, skate on the surface of Dal. Meanwhile, the colourful shikara's are resting on the bank of Dal as the boatmen look insecure and lost yet smile and wait for this freezing avatar of Dal to end in the valley soon.

Since, this is the responsibility of the dazzling season, to be the sole reason for change of color in the entire ambience of Kashmir valley, otherwise, who else has the ability to take up such a challenging task so effectively. Thereafter, a realization sets in that the *'Universe is the authentic Alchemy'.* Thus, guiding us to, aspire and connect to the Universal trust that exists in nature; as eventually we are all alchemists in our own distinctive manner and apptitude.

✩ **List out the people who value the role you play in their lives at this stage.**

1)_____________   2)_____________   3)_____________

4)_____________   5)_____________   6)_____________

The point to be sure of during this freezing phase is to know if any trace or kind of fear still exists within; as this is likely to create blockages / hurdles for the future. Therefore, it is desirable, for each individual to outstrip all such barriers mindfully, so as to be at ease during this unknown silent winter phase of life. Further, the effort to align in harmony with the 'All' is to be cultivated and practiced regularly in letter and spirit to be in sync with each and every detail of life in general and presence in particular. Therefore, during this wishful winter phase explore compassion, humility, kindness as the 'new norm'; with an over all focus on **'SELF-AUDIT'** in general and **'SELF-ACTUALIZATION'** in particular. Thus, guiding each individual to the way forward wherein each individual is an active and willful alchemist here to align and be as an integral part of this progressive Universal Alchemy!

Therefore, this in the time for an individual to overtake all insecurities, self-defeating thoughts, envy, arrogance etc as these emotions are identical to or equivalent to the energy vampires, draining out precious and vital life energy. These old outdated habits, are now required to be set aside; as until now these habits have entangled the individual **and kept him / her** distant from the true simple, honest and humble 'Self' all along. The moment one is able to accept oneself beyond the hollow and shallow mask of EGO, fear, insecurity etc and be the torch bearer ready to spread the precious unique light of bliss and joy to all uniformly, who have been waiting patiently until now. Therefore, the resolution for me as an individual here in Kashmir, during this troubled time is to notice the challenges, complexities as well as conflicts of life holistically; take control of the mind and not be distant from the exclusive purpose regarding my presence here with the acquired surety, assurance and confidence by now.

Further, this winter phase enlightens the flame of empathy, healing and compassion within as an illumunated being who is the carrier of light here on mother earth. This may initially appear distant and difficult for certain individuals/group to accept this glowing flame wholeheartedly; hence, there is no point in wasting time in convincing the naysayers; rather it is important to maintain this dynamic and vibrant glow acquired with deliberate efforts in order to be with this intense, rejuvenating and enthusiastic flow of life in line with the pristine Dal who has witnessed the defeat as well as the glory in past with profound composure and elegance.

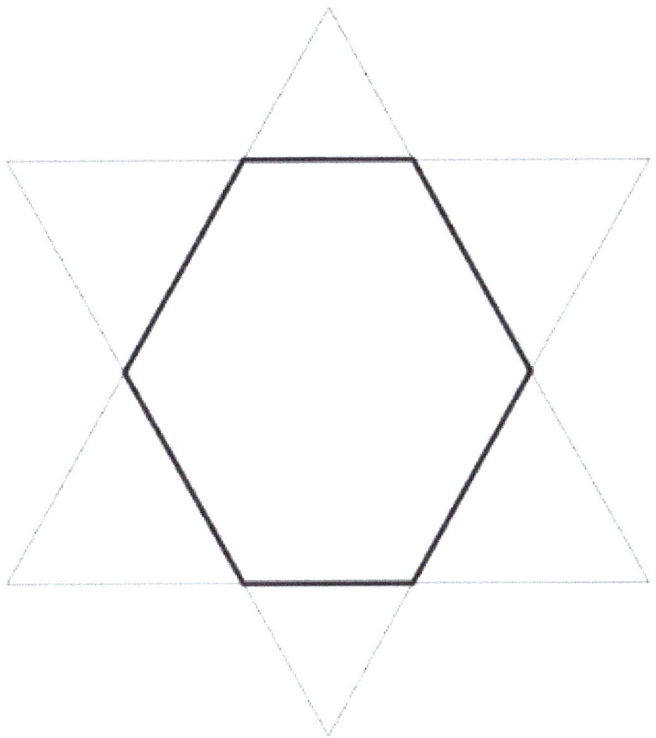

Write the things you need to let go *unconditionaly* on the outer tringle of the star.

Eventually this spirit of Universal co-existence gradually overtakes the emotion of rivalry, personal ambition and the endless wants/ desires to be with 'what is' as the real challenge. If the mental soil of a growing up child is cultivated cautiously with appropriate nutrition and space for development of body temple and mind coherently, only then, the child can grow up to be a secure and sure adult with thoughts of independence, freedom and **true** liberation. Thereafter, one can safely conclude that the fear of God is not the beginning of the wisdom but the knowledge of 'Self' is the real wisdom. No wonder it is clear that;

"Only if we understand, *we care. Only if we care, we will help.* Only if we help, we shall be saved."

.........*Jane Goodall*

☆ *It is filled with EVERY possibility*

IT IS YOUR *FUTURE*

Impression of 'SELF' connectivity be like;

Since life is only about Mind and Matter wherein if you don't mind it doesn't matter, however, the 'Self' connectivity may appear as;

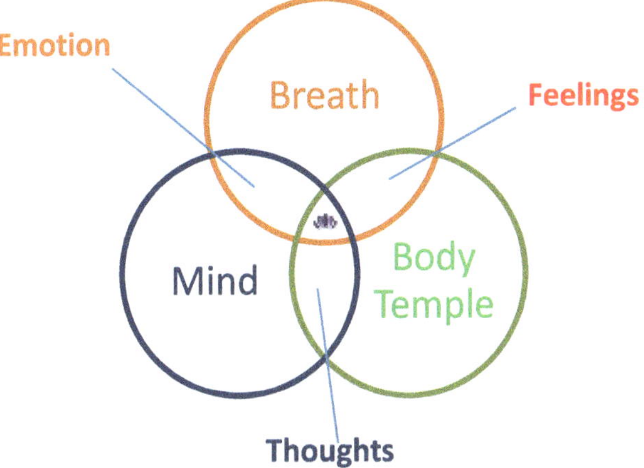

❖ Thoughts are the language of Mind, wherein Mind + Thoughts is mindfulness i.e. Balanced Mental State;

❖ Feelings are the language of Body Temple, wherein Feelings + Body Temple as Matter is all about the Physical Health;

❖ Breath binds Mind and Body Temple effectively yet flows effortlessly to connect to the Wellness as an energy in motion i.e. emotion.

Though this was a challenging time for the entire humanity across the globe yet being aligned with the flow of life made me understand the wisdom of winter as;

"Often when you think you're at the end of something,

You're at the beginning of something else."

....Fred Rogers

⭐ CLOSE YOUR EYES AND MAKE A WISH

a) **Why do you need** this wish to come true.

b) **WHY DON'T YOU NEED** this wish to come true.

☆ **What memories are you Grateful for,**

☆ **What experience are you glad to have ahead of you,**

Endless Epilogue

Eventually, it is an individual's vision to aspire and be with his / her own perceived and cherished 'Brand name', to live up to the 'desired Mission' to formulate a new 'Start-up' project to discover 'Self' with the new acquired skill and focus. Isn't it surprising to find that individuals are ready to trade 'Self' for a new start-up; which one may have started or joined and is working on the same yet completely distant and ignorant about the real 'Self' i.e. the real start-up project during this life.

Meanwhile, Dal is all along silently yet meticulously involved in expanding and diversifying its own brand name; continuously catering to the diverse requirements of the populace, thus, making each moment better than the previous one and focusing exclusively on sharing and caring about the need of the hour for all living beings here. Therefore, Dal as my sole companion here has taught me during my stay at Srinagar to;

"Trust the value of timing in life, just because someone has not yet figured out everything early in life; doesn't mean they are left behind or thrown out of life gear."

Relax, since the timing for each individual to bloom here is different and special, with adequate space for each one of us to blossom at our own pace. Whatever is unfolding at this precious moment at any given point of time in life is a sacred blessing; as at any given juncture, an individual is being prepared for a new and different challenge / direction. Further, each day in life is adding up more persistence, particularly when we are aware of the external surroundings; and not distant or caught up in fixing, controlling and manipulating life events and circumstances on one pretext or another.

As such being mindful and aware of the fact that *there are no accidents in life,* therefore, life events at times may appear like a mirage: which to a balanced mindset is at best only an illusion. All this and much more would be able to make sense to any individual due to the newly acquired awareness that he or she has willingly acquired by now; in coherence with the new opportunities to mindfully shift the attention from 'Wander to Wonder'; so as to actively participate and learn to live in abundance in every sphere of life here, thus adding up to the amazing life experiences, as;

'Appreciate the phase where you are in your journey. Even if it's not where you want to be. As every season in life serves a unique yet special purpose for each one of us here to adapt and grow with.'

Thereafter, the lessons learnt about life in and around Dal are the relevant reference point as well as important milestone to willfully consider what to allow in life particularly during the late spring phase and early summer phase as this will definitely be the stepping stone for an awesome autumn to unfold. Further, spending time with new people or partnership may be either encouraging and energizing or else depleting and draining the vital life energy in doubts, confusion, anxiety etc. amounts to wasting valuable time while ruminating over non-issues or the gaps that were left unaddressed earlier. The choice is with the individual to work on churning out the modified cud or to "dream high" than ever before.

Life therefore is only a gift, a present for all humans to explore and grow with, to harness the power within and connect to the 'Self' often with significant learning, unlearning and relearning; with appropriate time and space to introspect. Autumn is the time to be more assured of 'Self', being comfortable in giving up controls, to be with the unknown mysteries about 'life' in general and 'Self' in particular. The idea is to be empty/ idle more often, do less, yet, be present, aware and in sync with the external environment beyond the selfish desires of the Mind to be eager to explore not only the visible 'Self' which in reality is just a tip on the iceberg; would rather be enthusiastic to discover the 'invisible self' i.e. 'The Genie within'.

'The purpose is to make your inner world so strong and contended that no outer word or world can disturb it.'

As has been discussed earlier and known that during late spring and early summer phase anxiety, resentment, jealousy, stress etc. may seep in particularly when things don't happen in the desired manner as per the plan/wants. Thereafter, the autumn phase is identical to the "U turn" in life where one can mindfully address issues and resolve conflicts holistically. As by now the individual is no longer driven by the unfulfilled desires but has opted to be the sparkling pure gold, marching confidently towards the wonderful winter phase of life.

Further, the wonders of winter connect effortlessly to the energy of this 'Uniform Universe' where in "All is One" as "One is All". To be at ease with the impermanence and mortality about life in general so as to effortlessly glide over the daily nitty gritty of issues / concerns just like an eagle; be light and free as a vibrant, colorful butterfly; to enjoy this wishful gift called life.

Thus, the wisdom of winter teaches individuals to embrace, rejoice every sphere of life in abundance, be with the present beyond the concerns of past or future, so as to not miss any precious moment of this wholesome life that we are here to explore and grow with. As John Keats in his vision about human life closely mirrors the natural processes, reinforcing the bond between human beings and nature to live in a form that conveys a reverence of life's sequence and structure.

Now this is the time to give thanks to all including the readers who have been with the ideas, thoughts and views all along while reading this book at their own pace and attention; they are now blessed with a golden glow of gratitude that radiates warmth and humility about life experiences inside out.

An ode of gratitude to Life in general and Dal in particular,

Life!!

Human beings are born and they move on ...

However, life goes on forever,

The ever present transient flow...

Feel it, Live it, Experience it...

But please don't waste it,

As,

Life happens only in Now;

Where the past becomes alive,

The seedlings of future also germinate in now;

Life as a process just happens

Knowingly or unknowingly;

To enrich us, Guide us, Provide us,

The best we are all here on earth school to learn, absorb, grow and vibrate with,

Life has no contrast, no opposite and no pause,

It is a process to explore and be with here in now."

Take a moment to chose your own self energizing Mantra; that you wish someone else would say, write below

☆ *Write down all the things that are* **UNIQUE** *about you.*

Return to this page when you feel low.

Notes

85

Notes